A Man's Eye View

A Man's Eye View

Bob England

Vanguard Press

VANGUARD PAPERBACK

© Copyright 2024
Bob England

The right of Bob England to be identified as author of
this work has been asserted by him in accordance with the
Copyright, Designs and Patents Act 1988.

All Rights Reserved

No reproduction, copy or transmission of this publication
may be made without written permission.
No paragraph of this publication may be reproduced,
copied or transmitted save with the written permission of the publisher, or in
accordance with the provisions
of the Copyright Act 1956 (as amended).

Any person who commits any unauthorised act in relation to this publication
may be liable to criminal prosecution and civil claims for damages.

A CIP catalogue record for this title is available from the British Library.

ISBN 978-1-83794-239-8

This is a work of fiction. Names, characters, businesses, places, events and
incidents are either the products of the author's imagination or used in a
fictitious manner. Any resemblance to actual persons, living or dead, or actual
events is purely coincidental.

Vanguard Press is an imprint of
Pegasus Elliot Mackenzie Publishers Ltd.
www.pegasuspublishers.com

First Published in 2024

Vanguard Press
Sheraton House Castle Park
Cambridge England

Printed & Bound in Great Britain

Dedication

To all those who mended me. I give my sincerest Thank you and never-ending love.

Acknowledgements

To my family for your enduring love and support. Thank you.

A Challenge

If only I could win her heart, though cloaked in mystery,
A fair and precious gem, that shines, for everyone to see.
To hold her close, be by my side, becomes my nightly wonder,
This frog, a prince would sooner be, to win her with his thunder.
A brave and noble charge, I'd make and take on all the world,
The battle won, then cry out loud, tell all that she's my girl.
For there are those, that hold me back, disclosing all my faults?
Their sharpened tongues and spiteful wit, would lock me in the vaults.
But I will rise above the rest, and woo her very slowly,
With kind-hearted tender words, I will win this pretty trophy.

A Duet

Lyric sounds of rippled waves, meet the sunlight through a skirt,
Dappled patterns kaleidoscope, as silhouettes and shadows flirt.
Secret whispers, touch the breeze, like silk on a velvet skin,
The silent smiles, the eyes embrace, stirring passions deep within.
Like tears of rain, from soft white clouds, drifting through the sky,
Moist lips that part in ecstasy, each moan, an angel's sigh.
Warm sand, a bed for duelling love, tattoos the naked forms,
Disrobed hearts, pause to express, the pleasure from the storms.
Parched rhythms, raise their noble heads, marking beats of perfect time,
Slowly, gently, reaching peaks, to hear this duet chime.

A Letter to Heaven

I posted a letter, to heaven, today,
I gave it to an angel, who was passing my way.
I wanted to reach you, but you're out of touch,
To tell you, I love you, and to say just how much.
To say that I'm sorry, I didn't understand,
The way you were feeling, or what you had planned.
I'm so full of guilt, and it won't disappear,
It must be my fault that you're no longer here.
I keep going over, the thoughts in my head,
Was it something I did or something I said?
Why? Did I not see, the way that you were,
I try to remember, but it all seems a blur.
I think of you always, you are on my mind,
It's not much of a letter, just one single line.
I couldn't quite find, the right words to say,
It simply says this, "I miss you each day".

A Moment at Midnight

A heart still raw, and battle scarred, was held in faith, then sleeved,
To see the words and dared to hope, this time, could be believed.
The siren wailed, and wrote so well, confusion ruled the head,
Tempting thoughts of togetherness, but she trampled them instead.
From ignorance, and self-delight, her medusas' head snakes charmed,
Caused this unsuspecting sole, ensnared, to be embalmed.
Cast into a sea of dreams, the seductive trap was sprung,
The serpent shook her pretty head, and showed her forking tongue.

A Motif

Closet eyes, that sit and stare,
Search the voids, beyond the chair.
A glimpse of you, appears in shade,
With broken lines, and forms that fade.
I concentrate, with every sense,
To re-compose, your elegance.
Imagined shapes, of perfect form,
Dance across the sunlit dawn.
My palette mixed, from memories,
Of past encountered ecstasies.
A blanket canvas, in my head,
Painting thoughts, of words unsaid.
Inside my dreams, inside of me,
My fatal lapse of bravery.
Teasing looks, revealed the truth,
The heavy hands, demanded proof.
The vision dims, and disappears,
As the loneliness increases fears.

A Mystery

I am a simple, humble lad,
No superstar, but not too bad.
There is a secret, a mystery,
Inside all girls, that I can't see.
Pretty curves, seduce my mind,
With sexy sways of every kind.
I need a girlfriend, in my life,
I haven't got, a loving wife.
She didn't want me, anymore,
I'm on this shelf, inside the store.
Our differences, were far apart,
I need to make, a brand-new start.
A pretty maid, with face that's fair,
A lovely smile, and flowing hair,
I know she waits, out there for me,
I hope to solve this mystery.

A Poet

A Poet is what, I'd rather be,
And sit beneath the willow tree.
Play with words from dawn till dusk.
To smell the blooms and scent of musk.
And when, the light of day, is done,
To wander home, and find the one.
Who waits for me, with smiling face?
A passion flower, in creamy lace.
A precious bloom, from watered skies,
All men would hold, and idolize.
I would speak, of Art divine,
And feel her body, next to mine.
Leave the world, outside our doors,
With all its beauty, and its flaws.
And in one moment, held so tight,
We would drift into the night.

An Angel's Sigh

With arcs and curves, soft shadows land,
Like brushstrokes, from a painter's hand.
A satin moon, seeks to caress,
And trace, your naked tenderness.
A light, serene, spreads like a flame,
And lays upon, your slumbered frame.
Embossed, around your slender shape,
Reflecting midnight's silent drape.
You stir, and rhythms, gently rise,
As parting lips, breath angel's sighs,
Each movement whispers, to my sight,
As I watch you sleeping in the night.

Sad Life

It was past one a.m., when you walked, through the door,
You stumbled and staggered, and fell to the floor.
I can hear your foul mouth, as you kick off your shoes,
Your clothes, are all tattered, and covered in booze.
You took of your coat, and threw it, into the lounge,
Blaming the drink that you buy, with the money you scrounge.
I will pick it up, and I will put it away,
And I will clean up your mess as I do every day.
I am battered and broken, my heart is so cold,
I can't stand this anymore, I am tired and old.
Your voice starts to shriek, the louder you swear,
Your clumsy bare feet, ascending the stair.
My heart knows what's coming, it's the worst of my fears,
My body is tense, but I hold back the tears.
Why? Have you changed, I don't understand,
All the love that I give, is returned by your hand.
The children have heard you, they cover their heads,
They quiver and shake, alone in their beds.
I won't let you harm them, I will stand in your way,
And take the abuse you dish out, night and day.
Your brother has told me, "Don't live this sad life"
I should leave you forever and find a new wife.

Through a Misty Glass

I see you through a misty glass
In a crowded room, that blocks my pass.
Moths have gathered to your flame,
Some singed, return to try again.
A nightly ritual, that lingers on,
Until all the saddest ones, are gone.
Your magnet, turned up to the max,
Sending perfumed signals to attract.
The endless clucking roosters queue,
But I watch me, just watching you.

A Voice

A voice so soft and sweet, it makes the angel's sigh,
The tender notes, on a summer breeze, whisper gently by.
Drifting like a dancing moth, around a naked flame,
Hang in the air, and float into, an ever-welcome brain.
A voice that's like the petals, from a wild exotic bloom,
Holds to ransom, this prisoner, inside a lonely room.
Floods his sole and seeks to touch, each and every sense,
Caressed the ears, with a passion, so full and so intense.
A voice, that sings and heard, makes him broadly smile,
Lifts his heart with banished doubts, if only for a while.
A voice seduces all of him, through moistened honey lips,
And like a gift from cupid's bowl, the man, he gladly sips.
A voice, that is like a babbling brook, full up to the brim,
With sunshine stepping on the stones, before it takes a swim.

All My Fault

Call me simple, call me dumb,
Kick my head, and kick my bum.
For all my faults, I can't see why,
She had to pick, another guy.
I know I'm plain, and a little short,
I know I'm fat, and like to snort.
I drink too much, smoke, and swear,
Leave my clothes on the bedroom chair.
I dribble a bit, when I eat,
I have bad breath, and smelly feet.
I made her buy me lots of things,
I pawned her brooch and diamond rings.
She cooked my grub, and cleaned the house,
She was, the perfect little spouse.
I didn't shout, and I didn't bawl,
Well, only twice a day, was all.
I didn't think, she liked the sun,
Going out, and having fun.
Shopping, in the rain she stood,
I thought the walk would do her good.
I take her money, but that's just fair,
She doesn't need, the fancy hair.
'Make-up' what's that all about,
It's not as if, I let her out.

I never work, and the grass is long,
I just don't know, where I went wrong?

An E-Poets Lament

To those of you, you know who you are,
Played your games, just a bit too far.
It was you, who called to me,
With flirting words and passion free.
I did not want, to have 'a meet',
Women scorned, are a dangerous treat.
I had no aim, with sly content,
No viper's nest, or couched intent.
The predator, is in us all,
Inside the dark, inside our soul.
Your language, that was paper thin,
No meaning came, from deep within.
Before the 'meet' you joked and planned,
To greet me there, with open hand.
But someone, played a silly game,
I'm not the one, to name a name.
I stood all night, and stood alone,
Dressed in black, face carved from stone.
A wounded wolf, you thought to see,
An invented label, they stuck on me.
Your spiteful ways, have made things worse,
Now I must live with this versed curse.

Better Today

Somehow things seem, a little better today,
My world isn't feeling, so dull or so grey.
Descending the stairs, I looked in the mirror,
'Was that a smile', well maybe a glimmer.
No bills in the post, just a note from a friend,
Checking to see, if I'm still on the mend.
There was milk in the fridge, and tea in the pot,
Which is maybe 'a first', knowing my little lot.
The youngest was ready, and half out the door,
And 'that' has never, ever, happened before.
Everything is peaceful, no rows and no shouts,
I don't seem to be worried, or having those doubts.
You're gone and it's over, I think I've stopped crying,
I no longer care, about the cheating and lying.
The house is all tidy, with stuff put away,
Things, really do seem, a little bit better today.

Bleeding Heart

This bleeding heart, so cruelly split, and deeply cut in two,
Leaks droplets, bled on carpets, once gladly stained by you.
A rafted soul, now cast upon, an open vacant sea,
Battered by the winds of love, and distant memory.
Drifts, in aimless fooled pursuits, collecting bits of time,
Sifting, through the evidence, of your slowly fading crime.
Masking shame and brooding, in this never-ending hurt,
Sulks in caverns, far away, from other promises that flirt.
They tease, and seek to make, this noble jester rise,
As fortune's lady passes by, gripping cupid's prize.
She disappears beyond his reach, forever, so they say,
The hidden laughter, points in fun, and slowly turns away.
What chances stand, this failed band of the purist given gold?
Scratched and marked, by closet lies, that never will be told.
Endless walks through tunnelled thoughts, of a dark and blackest night,

Vague mists of promises, fail to see, a welcome coming light.
Watching, while the world in pairs, hold an impassioned warm embrace,
Steps back in silence, looking out, from this cold and lonely place.

Bottles and Blister Packs

Bottles and blister packs, litter the floor,
Echoes that ring, from the slam of the door.
Naked and cold, no shoes on my feet,
Alone in this room, wrapped in a sheet.
The weaves of the linen, are bathed in your scent,
And soaked in the tears, I cried as you went.
Reach out, and touch me, please ease this pain,
Don't think I can stand it, all over again.
Tell me you're sorry, for the things that you said,
This emptiness aches, and hurts in my head.
I know you don't mean it, and I know it's not true,
Life is not worth living, if life is without you.

A Cameo

Perfumed words, walk and sway,
Gently tease, tempt and play.
Candled lighting, paints the room,
Softening shadows, brightening gloom.
Warm breath, passes moistened lips,
Fingers reaching, searching, grips.
Palm to palm, with arching backs,
Tensions mount, and then relax.
Secret thoughts, now mystified,
Feelings rise, and then subside.
Muffled sounds of scented lace,
Heartbeats speed, the handed trace.
Volume erupts, from a whispered air,
As purpose links, this silent pair.

A Brief Encounter

I sat alone, just reading my book,
I watched her enter, with a half-hearted look.
Then something, rippled along my thighs,
A stirring blood, that began to rise.
She smiled and asked, "Is this seat free?"
I answered "Yes" a little bashfully.
The restaurant we shared, is deserted now,
The crew are watching dolphins, from out on the bow.
Her perfume was drifting, up into the air,
Tempting my conscience, 'C'mon if you dare'.
The sweet cologne, was enticing my sense,
And the atmosphere was becoming intense.
I laid the book, face down on my lap,
To hide the intrusive, rising sap.
She sipped her coffee, but she seemed to know,
As her tongue licked her lips, so softly and slow.
With cool dark eyes, so bright and so clear,
She looked right through me, and witnessed the fear.
That she might guess, what dwelt on my mind,
The steamiest thoughts, of a lustful kind.
To my delight, she was feeling the same,
As her shoeless toes, played a probing game.
She secretly pressed, her stealthily led path,
Along both my shoes, and around, up by my calf.

With a dual intent, our glazed eyes met,
In silent agreement, our contract was set.
She smiled so sweetly, and then blew me a kiss.
As she rose to her feet and handed me this.
A note had been scribbled, in haste, with a flurry.
'Meet me in cabin six and don't have the curry'.

The Butterfly

I thought I saw a butterfly, the like not seen before,
I wondered why? With all this space, she hovered by the door.
Flitting back and forth she'd go, up and down the frame,
Flirting with the world outside, she played a waiting game.
The flowers in the garden beds, tried hard to make her see,
That, if she'd only take a chance, how happy she could be.
With brightly coloured petals, and perfumed scent so sweet.
They tried hard to entice her, and give her such a treat.
But she just fluttered to and fro, thinking as she went,
What did they want? Those blossoms, what was their intent?
Now, amidst the blooms there grew a plant, a scruffy little weed,
He loved the pretty butterfly, and would let her know his need.
He called and croaked, with all his heart, it was a sad refrain,
But she just floated out a bit and then went in again.

The little weed was full of tears, as he watched her flying there,
Just out of reach, not near enough, perhaps she didn't care.
He called her name, most every day, but it seemed to no avail,
If she would only land on him, he knew he couldn't fail.
To make her see that life with him, might really be that true,
He would show her, all the special things that little weeds can do.

Apart

Memories littered, with favourite places,
Six bright eyes, and three little faces.
Minutes and hours, flood days and weeks,
Mind in a daze, while the heart never sleeps.
The noises are empty, they have no time,
The world is full, but now nothing is mine.
The distance is short, but the reach is too long,
For these troubled lyrics, of this soulless song.
Chances were had, but the ways were lost,
The money was counted, but never the cost.

Candy Floss Promises

Candy floss promises, float in the air,
All sweetness and light, set to ensnare.
Drifting they bubble, and froth with dissent,
Flawed with no substance, and meanings not meant.
They spin their deception, dissecting the truth,
Filled with invention, devoid of all proof.
Speaking in riddles and rhythm-less rhyme.
Just treading water and wasting the time.
Starved of nutrition and laid in the street,
Cold hearted shuffles, from under the sheet.
A back turned towards me, and looking ahead,
Faith held to ransom, by words cheaply said.
Retracing the steps, and sifting through sign,
Blaming the deed, on a fault that's not mine.

Change

What made you change, "Was it me?"
Did I look, but just couldn't see.
How far apart, our lives had been drawn,
Our true love vow, now, so badly worn.
Was I blind, to the passing of time,
Ignoring the changes, and missing the sign.
I crumbled and crashed, when you said goodbye,
My world faded and then started to die.
The special ties that held on to my heart,
Lay frayed and torn in the cold and the dark.
Alone on high ledges, just looking down,
Where jagged rocks and stones can be found.
They call to me, they can ease the pain,
Reaching up, they cloud and cluster my brain.
Just one step further, away from the past,
Where future ends and I find peace at last.

Disavowed

The language of love, was so easy to learn,
The trust was given, and not needed to earn.
Confettied memories, now drift on a breeze.
Brushing the pavement, disappearing with ease.
Steamy filled passion, once burning so bright,
Repeated in faith, with a knot tied so tight.
Sweet tender moments, swept into the gutter,
All promises broken, now stumble and stutter.
Marriage a gift, from one to the other,
Dissolves into bubbles, when one takes a lover.

A Dreamer

There is a dreamer, inside us all,
With eyes half-closed, and not on the ball.
Head in the clouds, while losing the plot,
Wanting, the 'have', but accepting 'have not'.
Neither hero nor heroine, just being heroic,
Given 'a chance', but then go and 'blow it'.
Superstition and luck, stroll arm in arm,
One carries a banner, the other a charm.
Don't walk under ladders, or step on that crack,
Give a wide birth, to a cat if it's black.
Life is a risk, but don't sit on the fence,
Try it and taste it, and use every sense.

Fishing

My brother and I, went fishing one day,
We decided to fish, in the old-fashioned way.
A bent pin on a string, and a cane for a rod,
We were hunting for minnows, not mullet or cod.
We had crisps in our pockets, and drinks in our hands,
We cast into the shallows, from warm golden sands.
We heard someone laughing, and turned round to see,
An old salty sea dog, who was down on one knee.
"You're 'avin' a laugh," he said it in jest.
"You won't catch no minnows, but you try your best."
"Why is that?" we said, amazed at his doubt.
"Because! You silly daft buggers, the tide has gone out.

Erotique

Warm tongues wrestle, in the dark,
As trembling fingers, seek their mark.
Slow and gentle, ease the way,
Stroke the skin, to tease and play.
Hands held firm, caress the thighs,
Mouths are moist, breathing sighs.
White teeth bite, the inner lip,
Impatient palms, let the fabric slip.
Feelings press, the pulse within,
Filling veins, and stretching skin.
A noble column so full and proud,
Removed in glory, from its shroud.
Anticipates, with a head held high,
As the hostess moans, her battle cry.
Wet and warm, their senses meet,
And quiver from the growing heat.
A grand salute, to the naked prize,
Their waiting need, intensifies.
Crimson ribbons, frame a path,
Encircled, with a practiced craft.
Awakes the collars, restless sleep,
Aroused, the valley's chambers weep.
With rushing breath, the nostrils flare,
Exploding passions fill the air.

Entwining limbs, increase their grip,
As tongues re-wet, the drying lip.
Tender looks, through eyes half-closed,
As the mind awaits, what the body knows.

Fantasy

I lay upon, this lonely bed,
Thoughts of you, run through my head.
Your caress, unlocked the chain,
Where a bounded soul, and love remain.
Buried deep, inside the dark,
Wait for you, to touch, to spark.
Feelings, that make, me a man,
You are, the only one that can.
Flashes, from your hidden form,
Flood my mind, and keep me warm.
Remind me, of your naked grace,
My pulse ignites and starts to race.
My dreaming hands, caress your thighs,
Feels the softness that yields and sighs.
The lightest touch, with finger tips,
Seeks, those pouting, moistened lips.
A single kiss, can break the heart,
Or release the sting, from cupid's dart.
The scent of you, engulfs the room,
With passion flowers, in full bloom.
Your heavy breath, and deepest moan,
Stirred the blood, and set in stone.
The swelling flesh, and stretching skin,
Holding back, the seeds within.

Entwined, inflamed, we took a chance,
And through, the ripened valley, danced.

The Firing Squad

Set in line, six armed men, stand fearless, facing me,
Into my eyes they cannot look, and do not want to see.
The wrong was done, mistakes were made, and it's too late now to change,
Steps were paced, to mark the ground, each has got his range.
The rifles shine, and glisten bright, reflect the morning sun.
All too soon the minutes fly, and then their deed is done.
In that time when echoed sounds, repeat around this wall,
The piercing lead will strike my bones, I will shudder and then fall.
My wrists are bound with chaffing ropes, hold arms that would be free,
To wrap themselves, once more around, my lover's sweet body.
I'd whisper softly, in her ear, how much to me she meant,
In this short time, I still remember each precious moment spent.
My drying lips were moistened by, our last long lingered kiss,

Of all the wonders in this world, it is her that I shall miss.

Muffled clicks as hammers cock, executioners hold their breath,

Secret ballots already drawn, to choose the one to fire death.

My time has come as they shuffle feet, the captain lifts his sword,

I hear a lark, sing in the sky, as I go to meet my lord.

From Venus to Medusa

Each day that passes, strips the heart of a disenchanted fool,
Who stunned and bruised, believed in love, thought it would conquer all.
He took your hand and bent his knee, saying words that would not falter,
Then took your arm, and held you close, lit by a candled alter.
That day seems strange, and distant now, it is clouded by the past,
Yet somewhere, deep inside his soul, he knew it could not last.
The way he thought about you then, a queen an earthly Venus,
A bond so strong, it would not break, and no-one would come between us.
Time goes by, and changes things, not all was as it seems,
You turned away, your back to him, and crushed his youthful dreams.
His faith had always been in you, no-one would turn your head,
But you put on the Judas sheet, and slipped into a bed.

He had an 'Eve', that offered love, but because of you, refused her,
His Venus now is lost to him, you have become a dark Medusa.

Full of Knots

My life is such a jumble, all frayed and full of knots,
I'm not a member of the 'haves' but a leader of 'have nots.'
I had it all, a perfect life, and pleasures by the score,
But someone took it all away, now I own an empty store.
I knew the 'someone' very well, she was my special mate,
I gave her all the love I had, but she turned it into hate.
It takes two they say, to break a vow, and spoil a loving trust,
She tore the heart and soul from me, and turned them into dust.
Now that time has passed, I can see, it wasn't all her fault,
She had a partner in her crime, and they planned a joint assault.
In secret games, they had their way, and didn't count the cost,
Excited by forbidden love, all consequence was lost.
The partnership, that we held dear, is smashed beyond repair,
So I must look for pastures new, and someone else to care.

In love and life my heart believed, that it would last forever more,
Now I am all alone, with empty shelves, just staring at the door.

A Girlfriend

I need a girlfriend, in my life,
To replace a mistrusted, unfaithful wife.
She must be sweet, and all mine,
A lovely figure and a cute behind.
A beaming smile, and a funny giggle,
And when she walks, a little wiggle.
Sexy eyes, and honey lips,
With pretty nails, on her finger-tips.
I don't need a cleaner, or a cook,
Just a girl, with a stunning look.
Age doesn't mean a thing to me.
But not, a kid, or an OAP.
A woman, with that girl inside,
To take a risk, and enjoy the ride.
Jump in puddles, in the spring,
Whisper soft, like an angel's wing.
She can look, at other blokes,
But she must laugh, at all my jokes.
Be impulsive, and take a chance,
Sing with me, and like to dance.
Walk on the beach, or sit in the park,
A kiss and a cuddle, when the light's got dark.
To be a friend and have a laugh,
To play her cards and share my bath.

She must be somewhere, perhaps the 'Net'
I just haven't found her yet.

The Great Oak and the Willow

The Great Oak and the Willow, lived on the river bank of life,
Neither had a partner, not a husband, nor a wife.
A love affair began to grow, but was doomed, right from the start,
A river ran between them, and it kept them far apart.
The Oak he had some damage, and his scars were very deep,
The Willow, young and pretty, on her own, would often weep.
A little breeze, became their friend, he would puff and gently blow,
Lifting up the slender boughs, to aid the sweet Willow.
She stretched and reached her branches out, across the river void,
To touch the Great Oak's saddened heart, before it was destroyed.
The sad old Oak, with head hung low, and roots stuck in the mud,
Felt her leaves and tender touch, begin to stir his blood.
The Great Oak, looked across at her, standing by the stream,
To love again, this pretty one, was beyond his wildest dream.

He brushed his leaves, and puffed the bark, that ran around his chest,
He may be old and falling down, but he had to look his best.
He stood up tall, and filled the air, as his sap began to rise.
She is so elegant he thought, I can't believe my eyes.
Alas his dream, was not to be, as a cloud came drifting by,
And hovered just above their heads, in an ever-darkening sky.
The little breeze could do no more, as the wind of change came down,
And blew across the open field, and whipped along the ground.
The little Willow, bent her head, swaying with the storm,
Because she danced so gracefully, she would not come to harm.
The old Oak, was distracted, as he stood there tall and proud,
He didn't feel the rainfall, as it dripped down from the cloud.
The extra weight, had soaked his crown, and his roots were losing grip,
The harsh wind, battered into him, and he began to slowly slip.
The little Willow, stretched out her arms, across the river flood,

She could not save, the grand old Oak, as he fell into the mud.
The waters raged, and pressed the banks, then swept the fallen tree,
They carried him away from shore, out to the open sea.
The sad little Willow now stands alone, still elegant and serene,
She often thinks of him and weeps, to dream 'what might have been'.

Marble

A tiny bundle, of pretty grey fur,
Gave never a sound, not even a purr.
Could leap to a sill, that was treble her height,
Without any effort, without any fright.
Would wander the house, all doors open wide,
And clamber on cushions, to be by your side.
Stunning green eyes, that could bring out a smile,
Sometimes a nuisance, but never a trial.
Little paws with claws, that begged for a treat,
With her head on one side, and a look "Oh! So sweet."
Marble, we miss you, the house isn't the same,
We will remember your beauty, when we think of your name.

Hopeful

I am tired and hungry, can't sleep anymore,
The bailiffs and collectors, line up at my door.
No food in the cupboard, I've drunk all the drink,
Dirty clothes on the floor, washing up in the sink.
The fire's gone out, and the light bulbs have blown,
The three China ducks on the wall, have all flown.
The TV is broken, and the phone's been cut off,
There's a draught through the door, and a leak in the loft.
The grass in the garden, is up to my waist,
And the curry I made, is devoid of all taste.
I am a sad sight, all grief and all sorrow,
I hope it's a good day, with some sunshine tomorrow.

Last Chance

Rugged features, on the stand,
Gives a heart, with open hand.
Forever hopeful, takes each risk,
Fails to see, loves two-faced twist.
An inner beauty, left unseen,
A book-jacket judged, with nothing between.
Cold harbours seek, to drench the skin,
Pulls at strings, from deep within.
A tired soul, too weak to fight,
Stands on cliff tops, in the night.
Calls to the jagged rocks, below,
Hold me close, then let me go.

How I Did Cry…

When she left, "Oh! How I did cry",
Sat about, and wondered why?
Day and night, feeling so sad,
Knots in my stomach, making me bad.
Now the light, is starting to dawn,
All this time, I have just been a pawn.
No TV soaps, to bore off the pants,
No arguments, or raves and rants.
'Home and away' has got up and gone,
Oh! My God, it did make me yawn.
No Dorothy Perkins, or shopping for shoes,
No mid-morning markets, and buffeting queues.
No pasta and salads, or broccoli bake,
"Oh! Dear, Oh! Dear," I'll have to eat cake.
Beer in the fridge, where 'Complan' would be,
The page in the paper, is opened at three.
The crossword is finished, I made it all up,
And the only clean crock, is this handle-less cup.
So, all in all, not as bad as I thought,
I nearly spent ages, feeling distraught.
Well, I really must go, and hoover the floor,
I am expecting the lady, who moved in next-door.

Jane
(Thank You)

You held my hand, and healed my heart,
To bring this brother, back from the dark.
Who in his pain, had lost his way,
Wandering stunned, from day to day.
In deep despair, with tortured soul,
You gave me hope, renewed my goal.
Your words, repeat, "Of course, you can,"
"Leave the boy and be a man."
"Dig deep," I can still hear you say,
While on cushions soft, my head you lay.
You took my arm, and kissed my cheek,
With tender words, you gently speak.
You raised me, from this lonely pit,
Gave me strength, and let me sit.
To rest awhile, and catch my breath,
You pulled me from a certain death.
Where in haste, I would have gone,
To ease the pain, of this sad song.
Whose melody, is bitter sweet?
With the echoed tunes, of loves deceit.
Once I danced, with partner fair,
Her flashing eyes, and golden hair.
Who laid with me, and was my queen,

But failed to share, my precious dream.
She walked away, into the night,
Across the street, and out of sight.
Yet you were there, to rescue me,
An angel, who could set me free.
You tore the blindfold, from my eyes,
Made me stand, and realise.
It wasn't me, that changed, but her,
Another love, she did prefer.
"She doesn't want you, understand,"
"You must be strong, and be a man."
"It's over now, to yourself be true,"
"And face this world, as one not two."
Your frozen words, pinned back my ears,
The painful truth, brought on the tears.
But, now in time, I know you're right.
I bless your strength that made me fight.

In the Making

In the 'making', leave the trust,
Trapped between, the love and lust.
Trampled rushing, to the peak,
Obscured meanings, wills are weak.
Instinct forced, and brought to bear,
Devoured, by one another's care.
Consumed by passion, a tsunami rain,
Flooding muscles, and filling brain.
Beached exhausted, with honour sold,
Giving blind, to the bodies mould.
Before the need, and then relief,
Where is the spirit, where's belief.

It Masquerade

Worded rhythms, on the screen,
Stretched out distance in between.
Where calligraphy, can skip and play,
With overtures, that tempt and sway.
Sits all alone, in this sad charade,
Freed by the flirting masquerade.
Pause a while, to create a tension,
And electrify this chipped dimension.
No body language, to hide or seek
These vocal fingers, deftly speak.
'It' clowns around, the forgotten souls,
And offers shovels, to dig their holes.

Mi Stress

Green eyes, peering from the dark,
Pointing fingers, find their mark.
Slithers in, with a beaming smile,
Pretends, this tearful crocodile.
Crying 'wolf', into the night,
Full of evil, full of spite.
The skirted cobra, lifts its' head,
Exposing fangs, of dripping red.
Strikes the heart, once again,
Inflicting damage, causing pain.
I see you through, a misty glass,
The crowded room, blocks my pass.
Moths have gathered, to your flame,
Some singed, return, to try again.
This nightly ritual, lingers on,
Till all, the saddest ones, are gone.
Your magnet, turned up to the max,
Sends perfumed signals, to attract.
With endless clucking, the roosters queue,
But, I watch me, just watching you.

My love

If my love was a raindrop, it would fill all the seas,
If my love was a leaf, it would cover the trees.
If my love was a minute, it would last every day,
If my love was a smile, it be children at play.
If my love was a pebble, would be a mountain so high,
If my love was a teardrop, everybody would cry.
If my love was a seed, flowers would cover the land,
If my love was a penny, be worth more than a grand.
If my love was a snowflake, it would cover the piste,
If my love was a menu, it would be a great feast.
If my love was a note, bells would echo in time,
If my love was a sonnet, all its' verses would rhyme.
If my love was a rocket, it would fly to the moon,
If my love was a song, would never be out of tune.
But my love, is just simple, faithful and true.
My love is forever, and I give it to you.

My Wednesday Girl

Your smile is the sunshine, that lights up my day,
Your voice is the music that sweet angels play.
Your eyes see in me, a much better man,
Your words are my strength, and they tell me 'I can'.
Your heart's full of laughter, that's melting my frost,
Your faith brings me home, whenever I am lost.
Your curves and caresses, are all I desire,
Your soft tender touch, is the spark to my fire.
Your arms are my fortress, whenever I'm down,
Your giggles reward me, when I'm 'acting the clown'.
Your grace and your beauty, are all that I see,
Your love, in my world, is all that I need.

She

She the fields, she the sky,
She the flowers that make me sigh.
She the sun, she the moon,
She the stars, that light my gloom.
She the night, she the day,
She the hope, that helps me pray.
She the beginning, she the end,
She completes, the time I spend.
She the laughter, she the tears,
She the smile that calms my fears.
She the part, she the whole,
She the piece that fills my soul.
She the first, she the last,
She the memories, of my past.

It's Not a Contest

A gauntlet, cast on private ground.
Seeking answers, to be found.
Question asked, but not disclosed,
All made demands are unopposed.
Tease the quarry, lure it in,
Lay the bait, but lay it thin.
Tempt the secrets, be their friend,
Side step once, and always bend.
Rapiers drawn, to pierce the mind,
For being cruel, or for being kind.
Plans are made, the trap is set,
All crystal-clear objectives met.
Seconds called, and stand apart,
Holding shields, against the heart.
Back to back, opponents stand,
Lines are drawn, across the sand.
Man or woman, both must win,
So, let this love affair begin.

Plastic Love

Perfumed pleasures, fill the dark
Chasteless shadows, stalk and mark.
Clumsy signals, trawl the street,
Shifting hands and shuffling feet.
Narcotic thrill, to temper sense,
Hypnosis fools, the present tense.
Passion begs, the body wakes,
The risk, an opportunist takes.
Needs and deeds, confused by must,
To satisfy, this wantful lust.
Softened flesh, that yields the fruit,
Commits the heart to a prostitute.

Old and Ugly

I cannot sweep you, of your feet,
Too old and ugly, to compete.
Not dark or handsome, no eyes of blue,
No bulging muscles, to impress you.
No clever wit, or endless charm,
No tanned expression, to disarm.
Can't cook a thing, or use a tool,
Tried acting mean, just looked a fool.
My money pouch, is wearing thin,
My practised smile, remains a grin.
'Come dancing', isn't quite my scene,
Two left feet, from a wayward gene.
Others seeds, are tall and stout,
Mine are limp, and fall about.
Romantic thoughts, I had one once,
Caused a headache, lasted months.
I think it's best, I know my place,
When out in public, I should hide my face.
But, if by chance, we should meet,
"I cannot sweep you of your feet."

A Prince of Fools

Don't bring my tomorrow, can't face that day,
The depth of this sadness, just won't go away.
Lost and bewildered, I am stuck in this maze.
blindful and stunned, all my senses erased.
Where once, a pure light, would brighten my path,
These cold-hearted embers, now shadow the hearth.
I could have been king, with a crown full of jewels,
But now all you see, is this sad prince of fools.

The Muse

A passion flower, bloomed last night,
Took my hand, and in her flight.
Lifted me up, to heights anew,
We soared and hovered, then we flew.
To paradise, on out stretched wings,
She whispered love and special things.
Her arms around, my neck so tight,
She took my breath, I thought she might.
A lovely smile, that knocked me out,
A pretty mouth, with lips that pout.
She laid with me, and took me in,
Held my heart, and made me spin.
With every move, she danced with me,
And in the dark, she set me free.
As dawn arrived, the new day smiled,
Remembered passions, warm and wild.

Predators

Predatory angels smile,
Parade their wares, in single file.
The painted Rubenesques, descend,
Side saddles mixed, their genders bend.
Perfumed handbags, weave their spells,
These Esmeraldas, can ring no bells.
Sharpened claws, their talons poised,
Misleading men, and enticing boys.
The mantis preys, and snares the weak,
Hiding behind, a glass mystique.
Distorts all vision, corrupts all views,
Clouds her worth, with coloured hues.
Immoral motives, that slip the skin,
Devouring souls to suck them in.

Prelude

Drops of blood, like teardrops fall,
On frozen ground, when the angels call.
A prelude waits, with baited breath,
The silence stalks, each lonely death.
Stiff fingers cold, and resolute,
Reach for the endless, absolute.
A tiny beam, of hopeful light,
Stumbles endless, across the night.
A single beat, a peaceful sound,
Lays incumbent on the ground.
As a precocious minute, stretches out,
Holding back, a strangled helpful shout.

Reflections

The stream of life, will ebb and flow,
As seeds are sown and futures grow.
Cascading waters, create the fall,
Awakened from, a rainbows call.
A stain filled glass, lets colours shine,
Shedding beams, on yours and mine.
Beneath the tranquil, peaceful pond,
The rapids lurk, to test the bond.
The crystal drops, refract the light,
Turning dreams, from day to night.
The rippled surface, rings and frames,
Reflects, the painted lover's games.
Twisted weeds and murky depths,
Clouds the truth, till nothings left.

Rose Tinted Glasses

As the rose-tinted glasses, fall from my eyes,
Peeling back the white paint, to reveal your black lies.
Your twisted lips, leech the baseless thought.
And your promises shrivel, now that you're caught.
Your pedestal weakens, it topples and falls,
'a deceiver', is scribbled, on bare naked walls.
Crystal clear plans, made from dreams in the night,
Are scratched on the surface, and doleful of light.
The embers of passion, ice cold in the sun,
Dormant and lifeless, all expectancies done.
Your transparent sole, with a heart full of booze,
Has nothing to win, but now, all to lose.

A Rush of Blood

Anticipate the rush of blood,
Its' rising tide, and deepest flood,
Sweating palms, of laboured trials,
Leading to, the bed of smiles.
Gently touched, the satin skin,
With tender curves, luring in.
Muted whispers, in the night,
Calm the fears, and make it right.
Scented sprays, cloud the room,
Stirring senses, in the gloom.
Love's music leaps, to set in stone,
The rigid form, from a tandem moan.
The rhythms, of a need entwined,
Breaking threads that tightly bind.
'Is this right', the question asked,
Lifting guilt, from the moment passed.
Urgent need, then takes the helm,
Steers the way, and leads the realm.
The conscience, is lagging far behind,
Convincing both, that it is 'time'.
Increasing thoughts, of a chaste refrain,
Be still, as the quenchless thirsts regain.
Set firm, despite the nagging doubt,
That almost puts, the fires out.

The ring-less fingers, intertwine,
With eyes that meet, and softly shine.
Knows the passion, can't be swayed,
And the given promise, won't be stayed.
Cheek to cheek, the dance begins,
Ignoring thoughts, of wrongful sins.
The time is right, emotions high,
Young doves, are learning 'how to fly'.
Fingered thumbs, grope in the dark,
Unpracticed fumbles, miss their mark.
Trembling hearts, and hands undress,
Twin pleasures seek their nakedness.
Covered bands, that slip away,
And fall to ground in silent play.
Pausing, finds the awkward clasp,
Breaking threads, that hold it fast,
Innocence, of forgotten youth,
Now stripped away, reveals the truth.
Matured, the clefted velvet crowns,
Of crescent form, much fuller now.
Rise and fall, their firmness proud,
Uncovered, from their silky shroud.
Entranced, the pulsing rapid beat,
Pounds the heart, as quick lips meet.
Two restless bodies, form a mesh,
Stretching skin, and hardening flesh.
A column rises, reaching up,
Dripping passion, from cupid's cup.
Seeks the prize, from private places,
As the crimson ribbon re-embraces.

Probes, each tactile, secret tongue,
Promotes the adult from the young.
Skin to skin, the saplings rock,
The limbs and bodies, interlock.
Bend together, with the breeze,
Mirrored moments, traced with ease.
Pull is pushed, with altered speeds,
Impatience cries, for desires needs.
Reaching points, of no return,
Their mixed emotions, fiercely burn.
Questions asked, for the second time,
What price to pay, for natures crime.
If just one arrow, from the flight,
Finds its' way, to pierce this night.
Scarlet stains, may spread the news,
Tells the tale, of this cupid cruise,
Torn the skin, a broken drum,
A learning curve, and lesson done.
All spent and gone, the pleasure passed,
Twin craft, becalmed, with folded mast.
Lay beached and resting, on the shore,
The innocence of youth no more.

The Sands of Time

Inscribed across, the sands of time,
This echoed story, is all mine.
Re-captured from a mirrored life,
Stands this man, without a wife.
Sleeps alone, with dreams so full,
Of future pleasures, when they call.
No longer tortured, by the past,
From broken chains, is running fast.
To gather, all those minutes lost,
Without a thought, or counting cost.
To see the sun, and touch the rain,
To find the strength, to banish pain.
Emerge a king, without a realm,
A ship-less captain, at the helm.
No tramp, no vagabond or rogue,
To set new fashions, to be in vogue.
A new world knocks, upon the door,
A wondrous place, I should explore.
I face this time, now standing tall,
No-one will ever, make me fall.

Sea of Dreams

Dripping poison down the phone,
Laced with a honeysuckle tone.
Scarab beetles, guard her web,
Spinning a widow's blackened thread.
Hearts are held with sticky tape,
Have no defence, against the rape.
Inside the puppet, meets the clown,
Walking planks, will let you drown.
Just drifting, on the sea of dreams,
The Crusoed souls, with parting seams.
The stirring cyclops, howls with rage,
And puts her pen, to scowling page.

Sea of Grace

White cotton fabric, loosely draped,
Shadowed outlines, curved and shaped.
A whispered breeze, tugs at the hem,
And steals a glimpse of naked skin.
Shoeless feet, step through the door,
As crumpled cloth, slips to the floor.
It fuels the fire, of pleasures dream,
Twin bodies meet, without a seam.
Mixing emotions, that stir the dust,
She the love, and he the lust.
Words exchanged, with a fluent tone,
Desires voiced, with a gentle moan.
Fan the flames, of scalded hearts,
By reaching deep, to feel the parts.
Freeze the time and alter space,
Rock the boats, on a sea of grace.
Stiff masted sails, billow full,
To seek the sounds, from a sirens call.
Wants fulfilled, and needs are reached,
The folded mast, becalmed and beached.

A Short Trip

I need a girl, to come with me,
To take a trip, across the sea.
Escaping from this moistened land,
To lay with me on golden sand.
I would treat her with respect,
Nothing back, would I expect.
But, if in all the warmth and sun,
She felt the need to 'turn me on.'
Then it would be, a fine romance,
If she could teach me how to dance.
When we're done, and had our wine,
I'd be hers, and she'd be mine.

Silken Veils

Silken veils that are paper thin,
Tug a watcher's, puppet string.
Poison darts, from a Bella's bow,
Pierce the heart and strikes the blow.
Hypnotic motions, freeze the feet,
A private dance, performs mystique.
Illusive glimpse, deceives the eye,
Distorts the vision, mutes the sigh.
Serpents tease, coil and sway.
And beckons forth the drooling prey.
Head first into, the lion's den,
To separate the boys from men.

The Smiling Serpent

The smiling serpent, twists the coils, of its' never-ending spine,
Around the soul, to choke out life, like natures coarse belle-bine.
New hands and old, reach out to give, a hope filled olive seed,
It falls between, the rugged cracks, of a hard and heartless deed.
Begging answers, that can't be found, from such a right-less wrong,
Hears bells of life, ring out each day, to a sad and mournful song.
Love's light that shone, on passions glow, is now reflected back,
A wedding march, a strangled tune, turns white to darkest black.
A pedestal of broken vows, lays crushed with every sound,
The empty plinth, once full of life, is trampled underground.
Voodoo dolls, stand face to face, portray the groom and bride,
Pins pierce deep, to loosen nuts and bolts of cupid's pride.
Then back to back, with hearts that turn, to blame all but themselves,

The love they shared, was paper thin, now lays on separate shelves.

A Sniper's Sight

With a sniper's sight, you crept behind,
To kill the faith, that I held blind.
Pierced the trust, we vowed to keep,
Now its empty bottles that help me sleep.
In the tortured darks, of wakeful nights,
I search the past, for wrongs and rights.
Guilty verdicts, that shift the blame,
Contradicts, a youthful cupid's game.
The eternal prize, of we not me,
Dissolves, in a fool filled destiny.

Some Memories

Some memories, like kissing bees, they settle on the lips,
Bring words that sting, and strike the heart, with venom on their tips.
Broken vows and shallow truths, that were never meant to last,
They are distant now, beyond the void, as they fade into the past.
From this loveless dark, there stirs a man, rising from his shell,
Cocooned in thoughts, and feelings now, that cast an evil spell.
Bare chests, that face a barren life, once cupped in tender palms,
Cannot melt iced words, with tenderness, or ever open arms.
To defrost the soul, and mend a heart, to bask in summers glow,
To bathe, by stepping stones of light, while temperate waters flow.

Was it Something, I Said…

My friends say, "Mate! Get a life,"
"Go out, and find another wife."
But, in my doom and gloom, I sit,
And wonder, "Is it worth the shit."
The first one, made a fool of me,
Let me down, and set me free.
Took my hand, some years ago,
Took my love, and all my 'dough'.
I built a nest, a grand affair,
A perfect home that kept me there.
We worked all day, and loved all night,
We didn't moan, and we didn't fight.
Holding hands, by a market stall,
A perfect pair, we were to all.
But then, by chance, the other day,
She looked at me, and had to say.
"You useless Pratt! I've 'ad enough,"
"Packed my bags, and now I'm off."

Stolen Time

Rustled leaves, play a minuet,
Sun drenched bodies, bathed in sweat.
Borrow the moments, and steal the time,
Factory and office, left far behind.
Precious seconds, picked and held,
Breaking free, from the busy world.
Touching lips, celebrate their prize,
Tender strokes, make senses rise.
Pleasures pink, moist and sweet,
Velvet alleys, crimson and deep.
Naked flesh, laid on the bladed reed,
Buttons are clawed, in frenzied greed.
Rhythms are rushed, to reach the peak,
Panted breath, on a flushing cheek.
The leaves parasol, this secret act,
As they quickly dress, and hurry back.

Stiletto Steps

I did not think of you, when you walked into my mind,
Stiletto steps, walk you through, crave attention and demand.
I'm having fun and feeling good, I'll get on with my life,
I've put the past, where it belongs, and no longer need a wife.
You did your best, to screw things up, you played me for a fool,
You took a man, behind my back, and broke our golden rule.
I do not need, your wicked games, or your practiced cold pretence,
I stand much taller now, and I'm putting up my best defence.
The time we had, was good and bad, it lays heavy on my hand,
Each savoured bit, of memories grit, engulfed by soft quicksand.
Those sad filled nights, and sorrowed days, are missing from my dreams,
There is a life, now after you, and a better one it seems.

A Sweet Assassin

My sweet assassin, in the night,
Pierced my heart, with sheer delight.
Turned my head, and teased my soul,
From broken pieces, made me whole.
With vixen eyes, this ram you tamed,
From boy to man and back again.
Cold sober dawn, awakes the thought,
memories, are trapped and caught.
Blind panic flushes, through the cheeks,
And knows, that you won't be back for weeks.

Sweet Siren

Sweet and gentle, eyes that shine,
Above the smile, from lips divine.
Whispered words, a tender noose,
Captures hearts, that can't break loose.
A web is spun from a gilded moan,
Entraps the soul, now not its own.
Repeating waves, against the shore,
The moonlight seen forever more.
Soft looks that dance, across the face,
Entice the hand, with a gentle grace.
Standing firm, the desire waits,
To push apart the pleasure gates.
Then slips beneath, a cotton shroud,
Awakes the valley, full and proud.
Captives caught in a lover's snare,
Are prisoners in the siren's lair?

Taking Her Glass

Taking her glass, he walked to the fire,
She was a beauty, his love and desire.
Leisurely basking, in a warm fiery glow,
Cold winds outside, were brushing the snow.
Flickering light, bathed and coated their skin,
She stirred very slowly, as she smiled at him.
Taking the glass, she sipped at the wine,
Music and candle-light, dancing in time.
Holding his hand, she looked into his eyes,
Pleasures aroused, were beginning to rise.
He slipped his arm, gently under her head,
Looking into her eyes, "I love you" he said.
Too long this man, had been on his own,
But now at this moment, he wasn't alone.
He kissed her wet lips, while stroking her hair,
Their bodies moved closer, the senses aware.
The real world, stepped back into the dark,
Dismissed by the heat, of a passionate spark.
Removing her clothing, he uncovered her form,
Heat from the fire, kept her nakedness warm.
They rolled over together, she on the top,
Consumed by each other, not wanting to stop.

Tears of Guilt

Tears of guilt, that douse a flame,
Point the way, and fix the blame.
Walk the walk, or drive the drive,
It is going anywhere that keeps me alive.
When I am moving, I am on my way,
To somewhere else, and another day.
It helps to pass, the wretched time,
That once was ours, is now all mine.
It stretches out from now till then,
In one straight line, no break or bend.
No day or night, or half past two,
Just the constant 'tics' that followed you.
The day you left, and broke my heart,
Our soldered lives, now torn apart.
The memories, of perfect days,
Soft lighted music and tender sways.
Whispered words, that brush the cheek,
Of the promises, that you could not keep.
Forbidden love and Judas fruit,
Rots the ground and kills the root.
Of that great oak, or family tree,
And all was born, from you and me.
Now lays dying, from the frost,
Empties the boughs when love is lost.

Where once we watered, arm in arm,
Seeds we made, and kept from harm.
Three precious gifts, of love you gave,
I held each tight, and vowed to save.
My gift to you, was love and trust,
You trod them both, into the dust.
You walked away, and took your smile,
And now this man, is just a child.

In the Alley

We went into the alley, it was cool and it was dark,
You pressed yourself against me, and said "Just for a lark."
Pinned to the wall, I could feel your warm, and silky skin,
The power of our passion, rose up from deep within.
Clothes were akimbo, as we took up, our balanced stance.
The pleasure did consume us, as we began our sexy dance.
We rocked and we rolled, our fingers gripping at our flesh,
The copper, he did shout, but all I heard was your 'Yessss'.
Now, I sit here, in chains, charged with a conduct so lewd.
I think, that I'm gentleman, and to refuse would be quite rude.
But from now on, I prefer, a bed, a mattress and a sheet.
No more for me, a 'quickie in the alley up the street.

The Wedlock

The wedlock picked and jemmied loose, is cast into the sea,
Abandoned values, drift in mists, from loves dishonesty.
Lashing tongues of guarded guilt, cut ribbons on the back.
As promises once set in stone, are chipped, and start to crack.
Each past regret, now mindful of, a past forgiven sin,
Waits outside the gates of time, and seeks a way back in.
The cupid arrow, barbed and tipped, became a poison dart.
In treachery, its' aim too low, struck a cold and faithless heart.
Inseparable, this partnership, made whole through heaven's doors.
Went its way, on bended knee, across uneven floors.
The sold deceit, and linking lies, form a chain around its mark,
A tourniquet that stems the flow, taking light and leaving dark.
Through time and tide, the mirror shows, a harmful want-less trust,

A precious gift, discarded now, with its metal left to rust.
Anger forges voodoo pins, from the corrupted band of gold,
As plans are laid, the future brings, a revenge that's best served cold.

A Trust

Crimson flames caress the logs,
Howling winds, duet with dogs.
Convulsing bodies, reach their peak,
Subsiding passion, taunts the weak.
Pleasured waves, stampede the brain,
And melts each ecstasy with pain.
The rush increases, pounds the ears,
Subdues the need, relieves the fears.
The heaving mass, of confusing forms,
The twisted limbs, and locking horns.
A final kiss, to seal the trust,
But who of you betrayed a trust.

Walking Backwards

Walking backwards, in the dark,
All thoughts and feelings disembark.
Each new day, when I awake,
Look in the mirror, to see the fake.
Cold blood flowing, in the veins,
Yesterday, still holds the reigns.
A stowaway, don't walk, don't run.
The re-tied knots, will come undone.
Mnemonic scent, of a faithless kiss,
Replay the times, of tenderness.
Black thoughts that whisper in the ear,
Create more pain, instil more fear.

White Witches

White witches, wear the blackest lace,
Can't look away, or turn your face.
The voyeur views, through standing stones,
Drawn curtains mask, the muffled moans.
The lost youth, stained in fading eyes,
The innocent fail to compromise.
Or is it just, the trick of night,
Vague shadows, dancing with the light.
The heartfelt soul is destitute,
From the bits of lust that prostitute.
Can't break the spell, or mystery,
Repeated in loves, lost fantasy.

Where Were You…

Where were you, when I was two?
And needed help, to tie my shoe.
Where were you, when I was three?
Fell of the wall, and grazed my knee.
Where were you, when I was six?
Being chased by boys with sticks.
Where were you, when I was ten?
I won first prize, I was clever then.
Where were you, when I was eleven?
My grandad died, and went to heaven.
Where were you, when at thirteen?
I was dropped, by the football team.
Where were you, when at eighteen?
I passed my test, and got a wicked machine.
Where were you, when I was twenty-one?
Misjudged the lights, thought my time was done.
Where were you, when I was twenty-three?
I met a girl, she is the one for me.
Where were you, when I was twenty-five?
And waiting for the stork to arrive.
Where were you, when I was twenty-nine?
Got 'laid off', with bailiffs on the line.
Where were you, when I was thirty-three?
I passed my exams and got a degree.

Where were you, when I was thirty-seven?
Watched my boys, play in the first eleven.
Where were you, when I was forty-one?
Depressed and down, nowhere to run.
Where were you, when I was forty-four?
Bought my house and a new front door,
Where were you, when I was forty-eight?
My son's engaged, he's found a mate.
Where were you, when I was fifty-two?
My world was broke, didn't know what to do.
Where were you, when I was fifty-five?
Happy now and glad to be alive.
Where you have always been, through the good and the bad.
Right beside me, my mum and my dad.

In memory of my wonderful parents, bless you both.

The Catcher

The catcher reached into his net,
To help a moth, still soaking wet.
He dried her wings, with tender care,
She flapped, and rose into the air.
She hovered free, for just a while,
Then turned, and gave the man a smile.
He blushed, to see her pretty face,
As she fluttered, back and forth with grace.
"I'm sorry, moth," the man he spoke,
"Your tips were singed, and black with smoke."
"Those droplets, they won't cause you harm,"
He said it soft, his voice was calm.
There in-between, the dusk and night,
Their eyes did meet and all was right.
He whispered softly, "What's your name."
But she had gone, in search of flame.

Young Love

Young lovers, in an empty house, are absent of all cares,
Rushed steps disturb, the loudest creaks, from ancient wooden stairs.
Flushed faces, search for sight and sound, with furtive shouldered looks,
And breath on tip-toe, as they pass, like burglars, thieves or crooks.
The trembled palms, reach out to touch a soft and rosy cheek,
A promise made, and now at last, this one is meant to keep.
The boarded floors shout whispers, telling tales, as they groan,
"Are you sure? Really sure," echoes in a stuttered tone.
The blush pink smiles, from pretty eyes, still young and still quite fresh.
Squeeze fingers to accompany, the solitary "Yes!"
The bedroom door creaks open, it seems so different now.
Carpets littered, once with toys, hanging from a mobile bough.
Laid out, in one far corner, lays a mattress and a sheet,
The realms of youthful laziness, now tidy, clean and neat.

The room is set, upon the stage, soon the curtain call will rise.
This play and this performance are the gift of nature's prize.

A Sleepless Night

Darkness falls, as silence calls,
Shadows play on papered walls.
Moonlight seeps, through curtain seams,
Disturbing, restless lucid dreams.
Relentless grunts, of a partner's sleep,
Duets with boards, that constant creak.
Pillows hard, and then too soft,
Something scurries, in the loft.
Bats or mice, it's hard to tell,
As imagination weaves its' spell.
Giant rats, with sharpened fangs,
Face each other, like teenage gangs.
The clocking *'tic'* that waits for *'toc'*
Dodges the missile, sweaty sock.
Seconds twist, and stretch in mime,
Outlast their normal space and time.
Aching limbs, and ancient bones,
Dull, with heavy weighted stones.
Fidget, fret, and kick the sheets,
Disturb the neat, and tidy pleats.
Eyes awake inventing shapes,
That form and fade, across the drapes.
Eternal yawns, that come and go,
Dragging moments, "Oh! So slow."